Hartmut Wilke, Ph.D.

Aquatic Turtles

Photographs: Christine Steimer

BARRON'S

Contents

42 Fit and Healthy

What Aquatic Turtles Are Like

Aquatic turtles are fascinating creatures that display a variety of behaviors. And yet they remain wild animals even when kept as pets, and they want to be treated as such even inside your house. On the following pages, you will find a lot of information to help you understand turtles better.

How Aquatic Turtles Live

Currently there are about 300 species of turtles living on earth. They are the descendants of primeval species that in the meantime have mostly become extinct. These ancestors began to take over the world as early as 250 million years ago. The dinosaurs didn't make their appearance until some sixty million years later. Of the species of turtle that live today, nearly 90 percent are tied to a life near or in water. The rest of them have adapted to an existence in dry regions and are grouped together in the family of tortoises.

Only a small number of the turtles that live in water inhabit the ocean or brackish water. Most turtles live in fresh water. This guidebook deals with them.

They include species from the *Kinosternidae* (Mud Turtles), *Emydidae* (Box Turtles and Pond Turtles), and *Chelidae* (Snake-necked Turtles). The aquatic turtles include some outstanding swimmers that rarely leave the water, such as the Snake-necked Turtles and some Pond Turtles. But they still must bury their eggs on land so they can incubate in the warmth of the sun. Generally aquatic turtles are loners. If living conditions are tight, however, even different species temporarily tolerate being close to and on top of one another—while basking in the sun, for example, when there is no other choice anywhere around. Then you can see them piled up on a single tree trunk that reaches into the water.

The Perfect Adaptation Wizards

The world's inland waters offer a great variety of ecological niches, to which an equally great number of species have adapted. Ecological niches are distinguished as follows:

> **Climatic Niches:** There are many stages between the continually warm waters of the tropics and icy winters and cold waters. Turtles can stay in tropical waters for a long time without forfeiting their preferred body temperature. On the other hand, they must get out of cold water to bring their body temperature to the required level in the sun.

> **Structural Niches:** This refers to the great range of structural elements of a body of water, such as places for hiding and sunning, to which every species has to adapt. For example, a swamp in an irrigated rice paddy requires a different hunting behavior and a different means of getting around (as with the Yellow-margined Box Turtle) than a large, open body of water with lots of free swimming room, the environment of Sliders and Painted Turtles. On the other hand, Mud Turtles of the *Kinosternon* and *Sternotherus* genera use thickly overgrown ditches and small bodies of water filled with roots and dead branches, in which they don't swim, but rather climb around everything under water.

There are also age-connected differences that can be observed within a species. Thus, young turtles live exclusively in water, whereas later on some also hunt in the shore areas on land.

Only a few species have adapted successfully to a very broad range of climates and biotopes and thus become geographically widespread. The European Pond Turtle (*Emys orbicularis*) is an example of this. It inhabits extensive swamps, overgrown ponds, alluvial forests, and open lakes in Central and Eastern Europe, where it must hibernate. But it also lives in the beds of Mediterranean watercourses that periodically dry up, and in small oases in northwestern Africa.

Recognizing Adaptations

You can tell which environment a species inhabits by its physical makeup.

> As a special adaptation to life in the water, the eyes and nose of aquatic turtles are very high on the head. That way when the animal is hiding calmly under the water, only its eyes and nose pro-

Depending on their origin, European turtles have varying requirements for care.

trude above the water so it can take in the sur-roundings without revealing itself.

❯ Species that are adapted to open bodies of water, such as the genera *Emys, Emydura,* and *Chelodina,* generally are good, fast swimmers. The shape of their shell is correspondingly flat and hydrodynamically efficient, comparable to a pebble that has been polished smooth in a riverbed.

❯ Species that are adapted to swimming areas near the banks with lots of obstacles include the Common Musk, Chinese Three-keeled, and South-east Asian Box Turtles. Their shells are generally more domed. (For leg adaptations, see photos 1 and 2 below.)

1 GOOD SWIMMERS The legs of good swimmers have notice-ably webbed toes, which provide more speed in the water. Long claws facilitate climbing onto steep trunks and shores. The species from the genera *Emys, Emydura*, and *Chelodina*, plus the Painted Turtles, are some of the good swimmers.

2 POOR SWIMMERS Many of these have only small webs between the toes. Like the good swimmers, they also have long claws for climbing above and below the water. The poor swimmers include such turtles as the Common Musk, the Chinese Three-keeled, and the Southeast Asian Box Turtles.

3 LAND DWELLERS The legs of aquatic turtles that live primarily on land, such as the Box Turtles, are similar in their pillar-like shape to the legs of tortoises (see photo). In terrestrial species, the metacarpus and finger bones, between which the webs of water-dwelling turtles stretch, are regressive.

Anatomy and Sensory Organs

Shell

The shell consists of a basic tissue of dermal bone covered by protective horny scutes. It is thinnest at the contact points or "seams" of the shell. There the dermal bones grow in breadth. Species are characterized by the color and the pattern of the scutes. Many aquatic turtles regularly shed the outermost and oldest layer of shell. Under some light and water conditions, the shell can become covered with algae, but that is harmless.

Claws

An aquatic turtle's claws are sharp and good for climbing. Between the toes there are webs that provide propulsion in the water. Male Painted Turtles use their very long claws in their courtship ritual.

Skin

The skin of aquatic turtles is softer and smoother than that of tortoises because of their small scales. Soft-shelled turtles don't have these scales. As a result they are capable of "breathing" through their skin under water, that is, taking in oxygen and releasing CO_2. They don't need to come up for air. The skin regularly loses the outermost layer of dermal bone in fairly large shreds and is replaced.

Ears

The round to oval head skin structure over the jaw joint behind the ears marks the location of the eardrum. The sense of hearing is poorly developed; aquatic turtles hear only low-frequency vibrations, and they perceive them more effectively under water than in the air. The creatures also perceive vibrations through their shells.

Eyes

Turtles have very good distance vision and are thus able to detect enemies early. They don't see as well up close. The eyes are protected by a pair of lids. The underlying glands easily become inflamed in a draft and in dirty water.

Nose

Aquatic turtles have an excellent sense of smell under water, for they are equipped with a nose and throat with many cells for smelling. Scents such as plant juices, carrion, or a mate can be detected even in small concentrations. Even in murky water this allows the turtles to find their goal reliably.

Behavior in the Wild

An aquatic turtle's daily routine involves keeping its body temperature in an optimal range, looking for food, resting, and avoiding detection by enemies.

Loners: Aquatic turtles are by nature loners. Occasionally clusters of turtles bask together. This increases their security, because one of them is always watching out for enemies.

Temperature Regulation: Turtles are cold-blooded creatures that cannot regulate their own body temperature. They use sunlight to warm themselves. This works particularly well on a sur-

1 In basking, the turtle selects a spot where the rays of the sun fall as vertically as possible onto its shell and thus provide the most warmth.

2 The Chinese Three-keeled Turtle looks about attentively. This is how it detects both food carried on the water and enemies.

face that provides insulation, such as wood or warm, dry sand. Oftentimes all they have to do is float near the surface of a calm body of water in which the top few inches have warmed up significantly. If they become too warm, they cool off in deeper layers of water.

Searching for Food: Turtles that also eat plant foods, such as Painted and River Turtles, find their basic food near the shores of the waters, in the form of all kinds of aquatic plants. Meat eaters, such as species from the genera *Emydura* and *Sternotherus*, and omnivores such as Sliders and Painted Turtles, search in the water for their share of snails, fishes, amphibians, and carrion. Many species also eat on land when they are adults; examples include the Yellow-margined Box Turtle and the Chinese Three-keeled Turtle.

How Young Turtles Behave

Protection from Enemies: Because of their small size, young turtles are particularly easy prey for raptors and large lizards such as monitor lizards and crocodiles. They ensure their survival by living in hiding as much as possible at first. At the edge of the water the best camouflage is provided by the leaves of large aquatic plants, and they find shelter among weedy water plants and flotsam. That's where they also locate their food.

Searching for Food: Young animals are nearly always searching about for food. In the warm shore regions of the water they find lots of krill (water fleas), snails, and insect larvae, which provide the necessary protein and vitamins.

Are Aquatic Turtles the Right Choice for You?

If you are a beginner at keeping turtles, I advise you to study this handbook before getting one. As a second step I recommend visiting a terrarium club near where you live. There you will meet owners and breeders and get an idea from the presentations about the kind of care aquatic turtles require.

Take a Test!

With many aquatic turtles, the life expectancy in the wild is from 40 to 60, or even up to 100 years. So before you get a species that lives to an old age and requires many years of care, I invite you to answer the following questions. If you answer "no" several times, then you should seriously reconsider your project.

› An aquarium with a capacity of 50 to 100 gallons (200–400 L) of water, along with substructure and technical accessories, can weigh 550 to nearly 1,000 pounds (250–450 kg) when filled with water. Can the structure of your house support that, and is your landlord amenable to it?

› For most of the year even mating pairs of turtles are incompatible. Are you prepared to set up a second aquarium for the partner? And even a third one for raising the young?

› Are you aware that there are ongoing costs for operating the turtle facility, for food, and for medical treatment?

› Are you prepared to deal with a half day of travel for competent veterinary advice if there is no help available in your immediate area?

› Do you have room for an outdoor enclosure? It is not an absolute requirement for certain species, but it is highly recommended.

Rewards in the Form of Interesting Observation of Turtle Behavior

This is an important aspect of keeping turtles. With an aquarium of the right size that is set up properly (see the profiles on pp. 14–21) and a nice outdoor enclosure you can experience fascinating aspects of a turtle's daily life.

1   The Red-bellied Short-necked Turtle rarely climbs onto land. Only pregnant females bask fairly frequently on land and need easy access.

2   The Spotted Turtle often goes onto land. Especially when the water is still cold, it often likes to bask on elevated sites.

One Turtle: After your aquatic turtle has warmed itself in the sun, it searches for food and rummages through the whole area. Which hiding place will it choose for its daily rest phase? With animals that hibernate, you can watch the preparations and the subsequent resumption of activity in the spring.
Multiple Turtles: It is exciting to see if they tolerate one another and if the mating goes according to plan. Producing eggs and raising young turtles is the high point of successful living conditions.
Further Pluses: Because turtles can live to a very old age, you will get years of enjoyment from your boarder. And if you are allergic to animal hair, you have nothing to fear from an aquatic turtle.

Aquatic Turtles for Children

At first your services as parents will be required, because it is up to you to make sure that the turtle has everything it needs. Under your supervision, children age six and up are very capable of learning responsibility for providing clean water and regular food. Their powers of observation are often better than those of adults, because children devote much more time to it. And as time goes by, this is a help in owning and caring for a turtle.

Help your children understand that turtles are wild animals, and are not for cuddling; they prefer to be treated with some detachment. A turtle will often display its shy, wild animal behavior when it is put into the backyard pond.

Aquatic Turtles and Other Pets

If you have a dog or a cat, you cannot leave these animals alone with your turtle. Dogs like to gnaw on turtles if they fit into their mouth, or they simply push them around on the ground, which is very stressful for your turtle. Cats often do the same thing. As one breeder told me, her friend's cat was peaceable as long as she was present. But as soon as the cat and turtle were left alone, the feline fished the turtle out of the terrarium and played soccer with it. Even rats, ferrets, and parrots could be interested in young turtles. Hamsters, guinea pigs, mice, and songbirds should pose no danger.

Only under supervision: A dog can injure your turtle seriously if left alone with it.

When You Go Away for Vacation

Find a knowledgeable person to take care of your turtle and enclosure before you go away for vacation. That will be easier if you already have some good contacts in a terrarium club. Tell your caregiver what your turtle is like and prepare an appropriate checklist (see box at right).

Notes on the Turtle Profiles

In the following pages I include only species that
> can be kept in our latitudes. The species that are bred most frequently and thus are the easiest ones to get are at the beginning; the less commonly bred species are at the end of the profiles.
> for the most part remain small enough so that they can be kept properly year-round in an aquarium or an aquaterrarium, in case you have absolutely no possibility of providing an outdoor enclosure.
> offer a real chance of putting up with one another as mates without stress and biting during the mating season.

I have left out species that require particularly elaborate care, such as soft-shelled turtles. After a few years' experience and study of advanced literature, you can choose a species that is not recommended here.

Vacation Care	
THE INFORMATION YOUR CAREGIVER NEEDS	
FOOD	Specify amount and type of food, plus feeding time.
BEHAVIOR	Describe your turtle's normal behavior. Also mention special behaviors, such as mating ritual or early signs of hibernation.
VETERINARIAN	Leave the veterinarian's address and phone number.
CLEANING	How and how often must the water in the aquarium be changed, the soil rinsed, and the filter cleaned?
MECHANICS	Explain how to tell if the mechanical devices are working properly.
FUSES	Where are the fuse box and the circuit breaker? Which fuses go with the setup for the turtle?
LAYING EGGS	Have everything ready in case your turtle lays eggs.

Emys orbicularis

European Pond Turtle

Subspecies: Thirteen, including *Emys orbicularis orbicularis* (Central Europe), *E. o. hellenica* (Po Plateau, Balkans), *E. o. fritzjuergenobsti* (Spain).

Protection Status: Check local regulations: Animals living in the wild may be subject to protection, and to prohibitions against transporting them to other locations.

Size: Males 6¼ inches (16 cm) on average and 21 ounces (600 g). Females 6¾ inches (17 cm) and 28–32 ounces (800–900 g); two-year-old animals approximately 2–2¾ inches (5–7 cm) and 2 ounces (60 g).

Distribution: Central and Southern Europe, the Balkans, Northwest Africa.

Habitat: Shore regions of all types of waters, including rivers and lakes.

Lifestyle: Amphibious, i.e., living both on land and in water.

Living Conditions: Can be kept year-round in an aquaterrarium. Water area at least 48 x 20 inches (120 × 50 cm) and 16 inches (40 cm) deep (= 55 gal. / 240 L) tank. Land area 14 × 20 x 8 inches (35 × 50 x 20 cm). This size is adequate for one grown mating pair during the mating season. Water temperature 73° to 77°F (23–25°C). If turtle is kept exclusively in an aquaterrarium, provide UV- and daylight. It's preferable to provide complementary outdoor quarters (see p. 38). Recommendation for keeping a mating pair together: Use two small, separate ponds instead of a single large one.

Behavior: A good swimmer, it also enjoys basking on land; sometimes shy.

Nutrition: Meat diet; in advanced years, very little plant food (10 percent).

Hibernation: In temperate climes, from about the end of September to the end of March or April (six to seven months). I recommend wintering under controlled conditions in a winter tank (see p. 50) at 41°F (5°C); according to experts 54–59°F (12–15°C) will also work.

Special Considerations: Outside the mating period, females must be separated from males. Eggs are laid starting around June, usually in the evening. Clutch of a dozen or more eggs about 4 inches (10 cm) deep. Incubation time just about three months.

If you acquire young turtles, I recommend that you get purebreds from a conscientious breeder.

Similar Care Requirements: River and Stream Turtles from the genus *Mauremys*, some species of which may be protected. In comparison with the European Pond Turtle, offspring are rather uncommon in river and stream turtles of this genus.

Emydura subglobosa
Red-bellied
Short-necked Turtle

Subspecies: Two (depending on source): *Emydura subglobosa subglobosa* and *E. s. worrelii*.
Protection status: None.
Size: Males, an average of about 6½ inches (17 cm), females 7 inches (18 cm), two-year-old turtle about 4 inches (10 cm). Turtles whose ancestors came from Australia may grow to be slightly larger (10 inches / 25 cm).
Distribution: Southern New Guinea and neighboring northern tip of Australia (Cape York, Jardine River, and tributaries).
Habitat: Large bodies of water (lakes and rivers).
Lifestyle: Aquatic—in other words, living in open water.
Living Conditions: Can be kept on land only in full summer when it's hot and in protected area; otherwise year-round in an aquarium with an area of at least 20 by 60 inches (50 × 150 cm) and 15 inches (40 cm) of water (= 70 gal. / 300 L tank) for one or two turtles. Land area for laying eggs 16 x 20 x 8 inches (40 × 50 × 20 cm). Water temperature 77°F (25°C) from November to February, which corresponds to the Australian winter (June–September)—the animals adapt easily—and 80°F (27°C) for the rest of the year. Set the daytime air temperature around two degrees higher than the water temperature. With turtles that are kept exclusively in an aquarium, UV- and daylight must be supplied. The illuminated area depends on the turtle's favorite resting place, but can also cover the water if the turtle likes to bask on the surface of the water.
Behavior: Very good swimmer, rarely stays on land; is sometimes shy.
Nutrition: Young animals need daily meat such as krill or insects and their larvae. Adolescents and adults need more plant food (varied diet). Composition and amount change daily. Good eaters with ceaseless appetite; thus, with older creatures, every other day observe a day of fasting with only light "appetizers" that provide more activity than calories. Check the turtle's weight!
Special Considerations: Interesting courtship behavior, in which the couple establish head contact before mating, and the male nods his head and "fans" the female's head with his foreleg. From April to June about seven to ten eggs per clutch. Several clutches per year are possible. Incubation period six to seven weeks at 82°F (28°C). Side-necked Turtles (see "Special Considerations" of Side-necked Turtles, p.18)
Similar Care Requirements: Southern Painted Turtles (*Chrysemys picta dorsalis*): males 4½ inches (11 cm), females 5½ inches (14 cm); however, the species needs more light and the use of a spotlight.

Sternotherus odoratus

Common Musk Turtle, Stinkpot

Subspecies: None.

Protection Status: Threatened in some areas of the United States.

Size: Males an average of up to 4 inches (10 cm), females up to 3½ inches (9 cm).

Distribution: From southeastern Canada and the eastern United States as far south as Florida.

Habitat: Soft bottoms of still and gently flowing waters with lots of roots, stones, and other underwater formations.

Lifestyle: Lives in the water near the shore; rarely comes onto land.

Living Conditions: Keep singly in an aquaterrarium with about an inch (2.5 cm) of sand on the bottom; area of 16 × 40 inches (40 × 100 cm) and 20 inches (50 cm) high (= 45 gal. / 200 L tank); water level for adult turtles: 10 to 12 inches (25–30 cm; corresponds to approx. 25 gal. / 100 L); water level for young turtles 4 to 6 inches (10–15 cm; corresponds to 9–14 gal. / 40–60 L of water). Land area for laying eggs, about 16 × 12 × 5 inches (40 × 30 × 12 cm). Water temperature 77°F (25°C), air temperature approx. 79–81°F (26–27°C). This turtle rarely basks, and only right under the surface of the water, where daylight and UV rays can penetrate. To get air the turtle needs climbing aids (see p. 31). Common Musk Turtles prefer underwater caves with easy access to the surface for hiding places, such as a cork tube (see p. 37).

Behavior: Is active at twilight. Stays in hiding during the day. Walks along the bottom of the body of water, climbs up to the top of the water. Does not like to swim.

Nutrition: Meat diet. Young animals need this daily; adolescent and adult animals are increasingly kept with interspersed days of fasting. Place food on the bottom of the body of water, where feeding takes place, plus on the shore, where "flying food" (such as crickets) drifts onto the water. Good eaters with perpetual appetite; thus, every other day observe a day of fasting for adult animals, with only small "appetizers" that provide more activity than nourishment. Keep an eye on the turtle's weight!

Hibernation: The farther north the turtle's origin, the earlier it will go into hibernation (observe its behavior; see p. 50). As needed, hibernation from November through February (two to three months) at 41 to 50°F (5–10°C). The animals spend the winter on land in damp bark mulch; this means that the humidity in the hibernation box must exceed 90 percent. Sensitive to drying out.

Special Considerations: If you have a mating pair, you have to keep them apart at times other than the mating season. Clutch with two to four eggs; gestation period 11 to 12 weeks. At the time of hatching the newborns are no larger than a cockchafer beetle.

Chinemys reevesii

Reeve's Turtle or Chinese Three-keeled Pond Turtle

Subspecies: Two, *Chinemys reevesii reevesii,* and *Ch. R. megalocephala,* in addition to approximately 30 local varieties.

Protection status: None.

Size: Males generally up to 4¾ inches (12 cm), females up to about 7 inches (18 cm); local varieties can grow up to about 12 inches (30 cm).

Distribution: Southeast China, Taiwan, Japan, and Hong Kong.

Habitat: Shallow waters and neighboring wetlands.

Lifestyle: Semi-aquatic—in other words, these turtles live both in the water and on the land; as young animals, only in the water.

Living Conditions: Aquaterrarium, 24 × 48 inches (40 × 60 cm), 20 inches (50 cm) tall (= 80 gal. / 360 L tank) is adequate for two females. Water depth for adult turtles: approximately 8 inches (20 cm; corresponds to approx. 14 gal. / 60 L); water depth for young turtles: 2 to 3 inches (5–7 cm; corresponds to approx. 4 gal. / 18 L). Water temperature, 75 to 79°F (24-26°C). Many young turtles have ancestors from subtropical areas, so it makes good sense to ask the breeder about the living conditions of the parents, or to use a "temperature gradient" (see p. 26) to determine the temperature that the young creatures prefer. Solid land area, 24 × 27 inches (70 × 60 cm), with narrow hollows made from pine-tree roots and grass sod for hiding places and for digging. Basking place with daylight in a corner of the land to provide UV rays. Can be kept outdoors in a garden pond or on a porch from June through August.

Behavior: Poor swimmers; young turtles prefer to run under the water; to get air they must be able to get to the surface easily (see p. 31). Old animals also enjoy being on land. Young and old bask on land; young turtles also like islands from which they can quickly get back into the water. Peaceable with other turtles of their own and other species, which makes keeping them together and reproduction easier (except for beginners).

Nutrition: Young turtles need a pure meat diet. Starting at 1½ or 2 years they can also have about 10 percent plant food.

Hibernation: Depends on the origin of the ancestors (ask the breeder and observe); possibility of December through February (three months) in the water at 33 to 45°F (4–7°C), or lowering the water temperature for three months to 55 to 59°F (13–15°C) with reduced activity and feeding.

Special Considerations: Starting at six years the males often turn black, i.e., they are melanistic. Clutch with two to eight eggs, generally in June. Several clutches per year are possible. The young hatch after eight to ten weeks.

Chelodina longicollis

Common Snake-necked Turtle

Subspecies: None.
Protection Status: None.
Size: Males up to an average of 7 inches (18 cm), females up to 8 inches (20 cm).
Distribution: Eastern Australia.
Habitat: Swamps, all types of calm waters.
Lifestyle: In water (aquatic) near the shoreline.
Living Conditions: Aquarium, 20 × 48 inches (120 × 50 cm), 16 to 20 inches (40–50 cm) of water (corresponding to 55–68 gal. / 240–300 L of water) will suffice for two animals (two females). Males have to be kept separately (a 45-gallon / 200 L aquarium is adequate for one animal). Water temperature 77–81°F (25–27°C), air temperature 82°F (28°C). Solid land area, 16 × 20 inches (40 × 50 cm), 8 inches (20 cm) high (see p. 37), set up over the water and accessible via a ramp from the water. If the land portion is used for sunning, train

a spotlight onto it; if not, then light the end of the ramp, where the turtles also sun themselves by climbing halfway out of the water. This species rarely basks in the water, so you can also occasionally turn the spotlight off for a couple of days. Observe your turtle and keep turning on the light experimentally.
Behavior: Lively swimmers; generally only the females climb onto land for a sunbath. This happens during the time her eggs are developing. The land portion is used primarily for laying eggs. The sociable creatures temporarily become vicious during the mating season.
Nutrition: These lively turtles enjoy live food that they can hunt, such as crickets and crustaceans.
Hibernation: A decrease in water temperature from December through February (three months) to 59–61°F (15–16°C) is beneficial to the creatures, whose ancestors came from southeastern Australia. They have retained the corresponding genetic predisposition. During this time the turtles eat less and are not so active, and yet they don't really hibernate. Ask your breeder and observe your turtle under a temperature gradient (see p. 26).
Special Considerations: This turtle is one of the "side-necked turtles," that is, they protect their head and long neck by tucking them sideways between their upper and lower shells. The turtles regularly shed plates from their shell through growth rather than disease, and they may come off in large sections. Clutch of 8 to as many as 18 eggs; the young hatch after eight to ten weeks. I have been successfully breeding these turtles since the 1980s using complete nutrition from whole, freshly killed fish (guppies) and newborn mice (bought frozen at the pet shop).

Clemmys guttata

Spotted Turtle

Subspecies: None.
Protection Status: None in the European Union or United States.
Size: Males and females up to about 4 inches (10 cm).
Distribution: Southeastern Canada to Florida, in the eastern United States.
Habitat: Swamps, slow rivers, wilderness waters (marshlands).
Lifestyle: Amphibious near shore.
Living Conditions: Aquaterrarium, 16 × 39 inches (100 × 40 cm), 20 inches (50 cm) high (45-gal. / 200 L tank). Water depth for young turtles: barely 2 inches / 5 cm (corresponding to 4½ gal. / 20 L); as they grow, gradually raise the water level up to a depth of 8 inches / 40 cm (corresponding to 9 gal. / 40 L) for adult turtles. Always keep the water clean. Depending on the origin of your turtle, keep the water temperature at 72–81°F (22–27°C). During the day, keep the air temperature between 73 and 82°F (23–28°C); at night, turn off the heat. If the breeder cannot provide you with any information about where the ancestors came from, then I recommend using a temperature gradient (see p. 26) to find out what temperature they prefer. For turtles around 3 inches (8 cm) and larger, provide a fairly large land area measuring 15 × 20 inches (40 × 50 cm) and 6 inches (15 cm) high for fairly long stays on land. They need access to daylight; install a UV lamp. An outdoor pool is recommended in the summer.

Behavior: Must be kept individually, for even females don't get along well with one another. Turtles from fairly cold waters sun themselves a lot on small grass tussocks, or on dry tree stumps.

Nutrition: Primarily a meat diet for young turtles. Adults can also have up to 10 percent plant diet (e.g., water plants from the pool in the yard). The turtles prefer to get their food in the water.

Hibernation: Under water in a foam pellet bed (see p. 51). The duration depends on the origin of the ancestors: December through February (two to three months) at 45°F (7°C) for turtles of southern origin; or October through April (six to seven months) at 37 to 39°F (3–4°C) for turtles from more northerly regions. Ask the breeder or observe your turtles.

Special Considerations: Mating in the water only under your supervision! Then separate the turtles immediately. One to two months later, two to eight eggs per clutch, the first in May or June. In the wild, females become sexually mature at 7 to 15 years; males at age 7 through 13. Females can live to the age of 110, and males to 65.

Similar to Care For: Western Painted Turtles (*Chrysemy picta belli*): males up to 6 inches (15 cm), females up to 7 inches (18 cm). Keep in an aquarium, water depth 16 inches (40 cm). Feed adult turtles a diet of half meat and half plant.

Kinosternon baurii

Striped Mud Turtle

Subspecies: Two, *Kinosternon baurii palmarum*, *Kinosternon baurii baurii*.

Protection status: In the United States there are threatened populations, mainly through draining of wetlands.

Size: Males up to about 4¾ inches (12 cm), females remaining a bit smaller at 3½ inches (9 cm).

Distribution: Florida, southern Georgia.

Habitat: Swamps and calm waters with a soft bottom.

Lifestyle: In the water near shore.

Living conditions: Aquarium, 16 × 40 inches (100 × 40 cm), with a height of 20 inches (50 cm) (= 45-gal. / 200 L tank); water level for young turtles: 2 inches (5 cm) (corresponding to 4½ gal. / 20 L); as the turtles grow, gradually increase the water level to a maximum of 12 inches (30 cm) (corresponding to about 27 gal. / 120 L) for fully grown turtles. Preferred water temperature, depending on the origin of the ancestors, may fall between 64 and 82°F (18–28°C); ask the breeder and/or test using the temperature gradient (see p. 26). Put in thread algae, egeria, or mouse-eared chickweed as a cover. Provide a hiding place in the water under the installed land portion with foam cubes an inch (2.5 cm) square. Soft bottom of fine sand, ¾–1 inch (2–2.5 cm) thick in the water. Put in roots and a sisal rope with a diameter of 1½ inches (4 cm) under the water as a climbing aid to the basking place and for coming up for air. Place a log in the middle as a sunning place. The land portion should have a surface area of 16 × 16 inches (40 × 40 cm), a side 6 inches (15 cm) high, and a mixture of deciduous leaf litter and sand in equal proportions to a depth of 5 inches (12 cm). Access to daylight: Set up UV lamp over sunning place. Put some flat stones into the water.

Behavior: Fairly shy and calm. Climbs a lot under water; if necessary, can also swim fairly well. Peaceable, even in breeding pairs. However, they often must be separated because the male is pushy.

Nutrition: Up to 80 percent meat diet; in the wild, this turtle prefers water snails.

Hibernation: November through February (three to four months) in foam pellets under water. Lower the water temperature to 45–55°F (7–13°C), depending on where the ancestors came from (observe their behavior). Creatures whose ancestors came from South Florida (with an average January temperature of 61°F / 19°C) do not rest during the winter. Many turtles also take a rest during the summer.

Special Considerations: Two hinges on the lower shell make it possible to close the opening in the shell. Clutch of one to eight eggs in the spring, with two more clutches per year possible. The young, which are only ¾–1 inch (2–2.5 cm) long, hatch after three to five months. Striped Mud Turtles reach sexual maturity only at age five to seven.

Cuora flavomarginata flavomarginata

Yellow-margined Box Turtle

Subspecies: Two (depending on the author): *C. f. evelynae, F.f. sinensis.*

Protection Status: WA II, EU-B, reporting required. In its original range, it is actively sought for food and commercial sale.

Size: Males and females up to around 8 inches (20 cm).

Distribution: *C. f. flavomarginata:* Taiwan; *C. f. evelynae:* Riukiu Islands; *C. f. sinensis:* southern China.

Habitat: Swamps; damp areas with open pools; calm, shady running waters.

Lifestyle: Semi-aquatic—in other words, they live both on land and in the water; young animals live exclusively in the water.

Living Conditions: Aquaterrarium 24 × 60 inches (60 × 150 cm) and 24 inches (60 cm) high (= 150 gal. / 540 L tank). Maximum water depth approximately 5 inches (12 cm), corresponding to 10 gallons / 36 L of water, for the turtles must be able to raise their heads easily above the surface of the water when they are standing on the bottom. A small filter with a "waterfall" that sets up a countercurrent provides a relative air humidity of more than 60 percent. Water temperature between 73 and 82°F (23–28°C). Use the temperature gradient (see p. 26) to determine the preferred temperature. During the day, air temperature 73 to 86°F (23–30°C), at night, 72 to 75°F (22–24°C). Land portion 24 × 40 inches (60 × 100 cm), 8 inches (20 cm) high. Provide comfortable access to land portion through branches or steps made of flat rocks. Land portion should have clumps of grasses and cork tubes, plus plenty of leafy plants for hiding. Direct the heat lamp partly onto the ramp, and partly onto the land portion. Access to daylight: Install a UV lamp. In the summer, may be kept on open land; then keep in an open-air enclosure for tortoises with a swimming area of appropriate size.

Behavior: Is rather shy. Many variations of courtship ritual, and mating both on land and in the water. Keep singly, since these turtles generally are quarrelsome.

Nutrition: Primarily meat diet, 10 percent supplement of ripe fruits such as bananas, kiwis, oranges, and watermelon. Feed turtles on the land portion.

Hibernation: December through January (two months) at 63–65°F (17–18°C) in a hibernation box (see p. 51); this is a prerequisite for reproduction.

Special Considerations: Two hinges on the lower shell make it possible to close the opening in the shell. Clutch four weeks after mating in the spring, generally with one to three eggs. The young hatch after 6 to 11 weeks and are about 1 to 1½ inches (2.5–4 cm) long. A second clutch is possible after one to two months. This species is the least commonly bred turtle in this handbook.

How to Get an Aquatic Turtle

You have made your decision, and you intend to get an aquatic turtle. But where do you get one? Sources include well-supplied pet shops and breeders. There you can buy offspring that have many advantages:

> They meet the requirements of the species and species protection legislation.

> You can ask about the precise living conditions. This is particularly helpful with species that have a large distribution from north to south and inhabit the various climatic areas that require specific living conditions. Examples include the Spotted Turtle and the Striped Mud Turtle (see the profiles on pp. 19 and 20). That way you get relatively reliable information on the preferred temperature range and whether or not the species needs a rest during the winter.

> If you get your turtle from a breeder, you will certainly have an opportunity to inspect the setup for the turtles. That will tell you more than a thousand words.

In my view it is best if you select a turtle from the species that I present to you in this handbook (see pp. 14–21).

From an Animal Shelter: You may be able to get adult specimens of various species from animal shelters, zoos, or collection locations, which will grow to be 8 to 12 inches (20–30 cm) long, like many of the Sliders and Painted Turtles. Such places take care of animals that have been abandoned or given up by their former owners for a variety of reasons.

Male aquatic turtles (right) have a noticeably longer tail than their female counterparts, and the base of the tail is broader.

Choosing the Right Turtle

Next comes the question of which turtle is the best choice for you.

Male or Female: The males of most of the species mentioned in this book generally remain smaller than the females. This could be important to you if the size of the lodging is an issue. Also, you cannot keep two males together even for a short time. However, two females from the species designated as "peaceable" in the profiles (see pp. 14–21) may work out fine.

How About a Mating Pair? Except for during the mating season, a sexually mature pair of turtles generally must be kept separately over the long run. This means that you will need two separate accommodations for a pair of turtles. I thus advise starting with a single turtle.

I recommend that you wait until you have three to four years of experience before building up a breeding population. Then if you want to breed turtles, but don't have enough room for several aquariums, find a breeding association where the turtles can be exchanged for breeding, and the offspring are shared.

Young or Old Turtle? Very young turtles are really "sweet," but taking care of them is a demanding task. A young turtle needs proper nutrition and care to grow up healthy and free of shell deformities (see p. 59). Soft shells and deformities are not particularly rare when the creatures are fed improperly, often with an excessively rich diet. It's easier to take care of a half-grown or adult turtle with a bone structure that has already solidified.

Bringing a Turtle Home

When you finally are ready to bring your chosen turtle home, you will get an appropriate travel container from the seller. It contains no water. Because of the anticipated bouncing, that would be uncomfortable for the turtle. Always get a detailed receipt from the seller with information about the turtle's species, sex, and protection status.

Young Turtles: Usually turtles are put into small plastic boxes (available from pet shops). A damp, absorbent sponge cloth makes a good carpet for the box. Take another sponge cloth and tear it into 2-inch (5-cm) squares and put these over the turtle. This provides a transport container with water storage and a cover (as a hiding place) for the turtle. With a closed cover you can keep the turtle inside from three to six hours during transport. If it is fairly

<table>
<tr><td colspan="2">

Good Choices for Beginners
</td></tr>
<tr><td colspan="2">I am often asked if there are any turtles that are easy to keep, remain small, and can put up with beginners' mistakes. Unfortunately, no! Still, I can mention a couple of species that I can recommend to beginners, and the reasons for the recommendations:</td></tr>
<tr><td>LOCAL BREEDING</td><td>You can get locally bred specimens from the species listed below, so the probability is low that you will get a turtle that is weakened or sick as the result of privation during transport.</td></tr>
<tr><td>CAN BE KEPT INDOORS</td><td>The mentioned species can be kept indoors all year without suffering any adverse consequences.</td></tr>
<tr><td>UNCOMPLI-CATED</td><td>Their living requirements are relatively easy to satisfy, even for beginners; in other words, they get by without excessively complicated technology and difficult feeding.</td></tr>
<tr><td colspan="2">THE RECOMMENDED SPECIES</td></tr>
<tr><td>RED-BELLIED SHORT-NECKED TURTLE</td><td>Advantage: No hibernation. Disadvantage: A large aquarium is needed.</td></tr>
<tr><td>STRIPED MUD TURTLE</td><td>Advantage: Remains quite small. Disadvantage: You have to test for the optimal temperature range (ask the breeder or test it yourself); possible hibernation.</td></tr>
<tr><td>COMMON MUSK TURTLE</td><td>Advantage: Very small, minimal technical demands. Disadvantage: Hibernation is critical.</td></tr>
</table>

cold or hot, as indicated in the "Living Conditions" section, put the travel container into a Styrofoam box with a lid.

Half-grown and Adult Turtles: These turtles are less sensitive to drying out than young ones, and they are put into a dry cotton bag with the stitching on the outside. This "bundle" is wrapped in several layers of crumpled newspaper inside a tight-fitting box to absorb any bumps and keep the turtle from sliding around. In the winter, place the box on top of a hot water bottle at 86°F (30°C) and wrap the box with a wool blanket. In my experience everything will keep well in the travel pouch for an hour or two, even in freezing weather.

1 THE "BUN" TEST: This is a way to see if a young turtle's shell is healthy. It should not give under gentle (!) pressure.

2 TRANSPORTATION HOME: Half-grown and adult turtles can be put into a dry cloth pouch with the seams turned to the outside.

Quarantine Is Important

At your home the turtle is first placed into a quarantine aquarium. For that purpose you can use either an all-glass aquarium or a square, black plastic tank (a mortar tray from a hardware store). It should have a capacity of 16 to 38 gallons (60–140 L), depending on the size of your turtle. For good swimmers, fill the tank halfway with water; poor swimmers get a water depth of twice the breadth of their shell. For setup and technical considerations, check the information provided for aquariums and aquaterrariums (see pp. 30–37); however, UV lighting is not required. If necessary, you can heat the water with an unbreakable aquarium heating wand (from a pet shop).

Especially for young Mud Turtles, the quarantine tank must be set up on an angle (see illustration at right) in order to create a gradual shoreline. Place a piece of rot-resistant outdoor carpeting on the bottom of the quarantine terrarium. That way the turtles will have traction in spite of the incline.

Why Quarantine? At first glance it is not possible to determine if a turtle is afflicted with something like worms or an infection. Even an honest breeder cannot guarantee this. After three weeks, if the turtle is still chipper and a stool sample turns out negative, then you can place it into its final home.

If the turtle is shy and hides, it should be allowed to remain in its hiding place until it comes out willingly. You can accelerate the process by providing fresh food every day. If it doesn't get eaten, remove it before the water becomes dirty. If you replace the water daily with clean water at the same temperature, you don't need a water filter, but you can still use one (see p. 33).

Taking a Fecal Sample: You should get a fecal sample from the turtle in the first few days after its arrival. Your veterinarian has special containers and can give you precise instructions on how to proceed.

Sometimes the droppings of aquatic turtles are so soft that they immediately dissolve in the water and you can't get a sample. In that case, place your turtle into the quarantine terrarium on newspaper and without water. This generally stimulates the turtle so it leaves droppings after a short while.

As soon as your veterinarian confirms that your turtle is free of worms, it can move into its new home.

Maintaining Personal Hygiene

In the past there have been some very rare cases in which aquatic turtles have transmitted disease pathogens such as amoebae and salmonella to humans. I therefore recommend that you wash your hands with soap and water every time you work with your setup. This also applies whenever you pick up your turtle. You should also avoid siphoning "turtle water" through a tube sucked by mouth.

Poor swimmers also need a gradual shoreline in the quarantine tank. A piece of outdoor carpeting provides traction and is easy to clean.

Danger – **Interfering with Nature**

REMOVAL FROM THE WILD: For many people, wildlife conservation simply means that protected animals may not be captured. In many places there are laws that govern which species may be captured in the wild; be sure to check local regulations.

RELEASE INTO THE WILD: But wildlife protection also means that it is forbidden to indiscriminately release both local and non-indigenous turtles into the nearest body of water. The Red-cheeked Slider (*Chrysemys scripta elegans*) is an example of the damage that such species can inflict on the local animal population, which gets displaced.

Acclimating an Aquatic Turtle

You can make it easier for your turtle to get used to its new home if you provide it with enough cover, such as holes on land (for *Cuora flavomarginata*) and pieces of bark and/or reeds in the water, as appropriate, where the turtle likes to hang out. You will not always get precise information about the temperature conditions your turtle prefers. Here's how to figure that out.

Determining the Appropriate Living Conditions: Many species are distributed so widely that if you don't know precisely where your particular turtle came from, it is easy to provide the wrong living conditions. It may be that your turtle is genetically programmed by its ancestors, who lived in fairly cold areas, to take a winter rest, and still carries this schedule inside it. But your species of turtle also lives in the warmer regions of the earth, in which no winter rest is necessary. This could be the case with such turtles as the Yellow-margined Box

Turtle and the Spotted Turtle. For you, this means that even if you see no symptoms of winter rest, that is not an unequivocal indication, for your turtle may be forced to stay "awake" by the warm temperature in the terrarium.

Testing for the Right Temperature

Science has not abandoned you to your own resources with this problem. It has come up with the "temperature gradient." It works as follows: In the water or on the land, you create a series of temperature gradients (similar to a row of organ pipes), and for at least two or three days observe which temperature zone your turtle prefers at what times, and for how long. Then you know its preferred temperature range. The test works well in the spring during peak activity and in the fall, for determining the need for a winter rest. Here's how to proceed:

> It's fairly difficult to set up temperature gradations in the water. You can solve this problem by putting in a tightly fitting Styrofoam wall (about an inch / 2.5 cm thick) into the water of the aquarium or aquaterrarium. The water has to reach the upper edge of the Styrofoam wall so that the little creature can easily get from one compartment to the other.

> For testing, select temperature steps of two degrees, starting with the lowest temperature recommended for your species. In other words, you increase the water temperature by two degrees

As in the wild, a turtle must always be able to seek out its preferred temperature.

Centigrade with an aquarium heater in one of the two compartments and observe your turtle.

> If the turtle spends the whole day in the warmer of the two compartments, raise the temperature in the other section by another two degrees Centigrade. But if the turtle prefers the cooler half, reduce the temperature in the neighboring section by two degrees Centigrade.

> Proceed in this manner. At some point the turtle will tolerate the next warm or cold step only for a short time, or not at all. That tells you your turtle's preferred temperature limits.

Tip: You can also create three or four areas using Styrofoam sheets and heat the sections of water to different temperatures. That's a quicker way to accomplish your purpose.

Results from a Series of Measurements: Doing this type of test every three months gives you information about the individual fluctuation range of your turtle's preferred temperature. You will also find out if your turtle prefers cooler water in the fall because it wants to take a winter rest.

Incidentally, you ascertain the air temperature in a similar way, but place the spotlight in the farthest end of the terrarium to make it the warmest place. That sets up a temperature difference with the unheated end of the terrarium.

Note: I want to stress that this procedure should not be used as a standard for acclimation, but only as an aid in clearing up major questions about living conditions at the outset, in case you don't get any information about your turtle's living conditions when you buy it.

Important Information on Species Protection

TIPS FROM THE
TURTLE EXPERT
Dr. Hartmut Wilke

If you own a protected species (see Profiles, pp. 14–21), the following conditions apply to you under species protection legislation. Protected species are listed in the Washington Accord on Wildlife Conservation and in legislation in the European Union. You can check online for more information about the protection status of your turtle.

COMPETENCY CERTIFICATE: Wildlife conservation officials can test the adequacy of your knowledge of a turtle's living conditions and care requirements. If you don't pass the test, you can take it again. Your personal responsibility can also play a role. In addition, you must provide appropriate living conditions.

REPORTING REQUIREMENT: Protected species are subject to a reporting requirement to the authorities who are responsible for your area. If you don't report your turtle, you cannot get a certificate for the legality of your turtle, and in some cases the authorities can confiscate your pet.

Providing the Right Living Conditions

On the following pages you will find descriptions of how aquatic turtles use various habitats, and the best living conditions to provide for them. I provide information about the general conditions. But within those parameters you can enjoy boundless imagination and creativity in setting up your turtle's home.

How Aquatic Turtles in Captivity Want to Live

As you have seen in the profiles on pages 14 through 21, the individual species of turtles pose various demands on their habitat, and thus on their living conditions. Many species of aquatic turtle prefer to live in open water, where they can swim. They thus prefer to be kept in an aquarium with deep water. Other species live in the water, but don't swim very well, and thus prefer to stay close to the shore. These species need an aquarium with shallower water. The last group lives partially in the water and partly on land. These creatures need an aquaterrarium with a large land portion. To find out where your turtle prefers to live, I advise you to watch it very closely right at the outset. That way you will learn to recognize the characteristics of your pet that you must take into consideration in setting up its accommodations. For example, if your turtle is quite shy, you should provide additional hiding places. If the turtle has difficulty reaching the surface of the water, it will need additional underwater climbing aids. Does your turtle prefer to sun itself and quickly flee back into the water? Then I recommend a suspended island or a piece of root installed in the middle of the water (see p. 31). As you study your turtle, you will also discover whether it needs a sunning place over deep water, or prefers a dry shore area and shallow water. In other words, through careful observation you will quickly learn how your turtle wants to live. Observing your turtle is also very exciting and entertaining.

A Comfortable Setup

The Right Tank

Size: The longer it is, the easier it is for you to set it up if you want to put in such things as branches for smooth transitions. Even a baby turtle needs plenty of room. All the size specifications in the profiles generally refer to single turtles. But you can also put in a second female or a mating pair on a temporary basis during the mating season.

Tip: Buy an all-glass tank without a cover and a light. They are not needed.

Location: A bright location away from direct sun and drafty windows and doors is best. Daylight should always play a role. An ideal setup is under a glass roof. The change in the length of the day throughout the year has a major influence on your turtle's biology. It drives the turtle's hormone regulation, and thus its winter rest and reproduction. Vibrations from electric appliances (refrigerator, stereo speakers) bother turtles, as do strong smells such as tobacco smoke and air fresheners.

The Right Setup

Bottom: Put around an inch (2.5 cm) of washed river sand onto the bottom of the tank.

Hiding Places: Young turtles in particular have an extreme need for security. They like it best when you put some pine roots or cork bark tubes (see illustration, p. 36) into the water; your turtle can withdraw to the hollows and corners. You can provide sprouting water plants or pieces of reeds and cork bark for cover.

An Appropriate Feeding Place: Depending on the species (see Profiles pp. 14–21), you feed either in the water or on the land. For water dwellers you don't need any special setup; the turtles that feed on land get their food on a ramp or from a bowl.

A Sunning Bench Is Necessary: Most aquatic turtles (see Profiles pp. 14–21) sun themselves as they paddle in the water, or on the water on floating wood and islands of reeds. Other species, such as *Emys* and *Cora*, sun themselves on land. In these cases set up an appropriate land portion (see p. 36) that is easy to reach from the water.

All Young Turtles Have Special Needs

All young turtles at first grow up exclusively in the water. If yours is of a species that does not swim well, lower the water level so that your turtle can comfortably get air when standing on the bottom.

Keeping Glass from Breaking

CUSHIONING: Aquariums and aquaterrariums are set up level on a Styrofoam panel (from a building supplies store) or on a more visually pleasing foam mat (from a pet shop). Make sure that no foreign body comes between the mat and the glass. That way you will keep the tank from coming apart from uneven stresses.

CLIMBING AIDS: Poor swimmers appreciate climbing aids under water; they like to sunbathe on them with their shell out of the water. Sisal ropes around 2 inches (5 cm) thick are better for decorating in small aquariums because they take up less room than roots. They look natural and are relatively resistant to rot. A basic tenet is that the larger your aquarium, the easier it is to set up your turtle's habitat, and the more attractive it will be.

HIDING UNDER A PIECE OF CORK BARK: If your turtle can feel safe from discovery and sudden seizure, it is much more comfortable, so always provide adequate cover inside the terrarium. You can tell by this Florida Red-bellied Painted Turtle's body language that it is relaxed. The need for shelter is greater among young turtles than with older ones.

A SUNNING PLACE: Roots and stones in the middle of the water are ideal. In case of danger this Mississippi Map Turtle can simply slide into the water.

Technical Equipment in the Setup

A functioning setup with all essential elements is just what's needed for the health and comfort of your aquatic turtle.

The Correct Temperature

As cold-blooded animals, turtles cannot regulate their body temperature by themselves, and they take on the temperature of their surroundings. So a turtle will want to find a certain temperature range in its habitat. This applies to both aquariums and aquaterrariums.

1 Glass aquarium heating elements are protected against breakage by means of decoration or a protective cage (from a pet shop).

2 A good choice is a heater/filter with a filter capacity of 12 to 18 quarts / liters and a pump that can be turned down as needed.

Water Temperature: This is regulated by means of a filter with a built-in heater. An adjustable glass aquarium heater can be used alternatively or additionally (protect it from breakage!). Because even fairly small natural bodies of water scarcely lose heat during the night, it is not necessary to turn down the water temperature at night.

Air Temperature: Always provide a temperature difference during the day by directing a spotlight (104°F / 40°C) onto the bottom or a branch in a corner of the setup. This creates various temperature ranges between this corner and the rest of the area. Make sure that the air never gets colder than the water. This can happen easily in the presence of a draft. At night the spotlight is turned off with a timer switch.

Thermometer: A traditional laboratory thermometer (32–140°F / 0–60°C) or a digital thermometer will help you keep a constant (!) watch on the water and air temperatures.

Vitally Important Light

Fluorescent Lighting: This is necessary if there is not enough natural daylight, for example, if the tank is in a dark room. This provides the basic lighting—for the plants as well—by means of a timer switch. The duration of the lighting is adjusted to the current length of the day.

Spotlight: This is always required. A 100-watt, 230-volt lamp with a 10-degree illumination arc produces a spot of light 7 inches (18 cm) in diameter, but a light intensity of 10,000 Lux. If you hang the light lower, even 60 watts may be adequate; give it a try. For Mud Turtles of the genera *Ster-*

notherus and *Kinosternon* this generally will be an adequate light source.

UV Lamps: This is always required when a turtle is kept exclusively indoors, for it delivers the UV portion of sunlight that is important in bone (shell!) growth. Even crepuscular turtles bask in the morning or evening sun. UV lamps include such products as the 300-watt Ultra-Vitalux from Osram or similar lamps from other manufacturers.

Halogen Lamps: These meet the light needs of Painted Turtles as well as turtles of the genera *Emydura* and *Emys.* There are quartz and ceramic vapor and high-pressure mercury vapor lamps. Quartz bulbs (150 watts) produce 13,000 lumens, which comes very close to natural daylight. High-pressure mercury vapor lamps (125 watts) produce 6,200 lumens. Adjust the intensity of the illumination to the season by hanging the lamp at a height of about 32 inches (80 cm) in the summer, but at about 5 feet (1.5 m) in the spring and fall. Only about a third of the tank—the basking area— should be fully illuminated.

Timer Switch: This is used to control all necessary lamps and devices.

Water Quality

Filter: Select a heater filter that's as large as possible. That way, even with small amounts of water to be filtered you get a usable overall volume. From my personal experience, I recommend a filter consisting of a combination of about 1½ inches (4 cm) of fairly fine fleece as a coarse strainer, plus a filter pad of the same material with large pores (from a pet shop) in the rest of the filter; the latter serves as a carrier for the microorganisms that perform the breakdown of dissolved nutrients.

Pump: This processes about 600 quarts / liters per hour. As long as the turtle is still small, you can turn down the pump (in accordance with the manufacturer's instructions) so that the smaller volume of water doesn't swirl around too much or even suck up the turtle. I recommend fitting the outflow in the tank with a protective grating available in stores. It's a good idea to have a glazer cut an appropriate drain hole in the bottom of the tank. A standard drain with a ball valve is installed. That way you optimize the discharge from the filter, and you will appreciate this practical way of draining the tank every time you clean it.

3 UV lamps are installed along with a spotlight. Twenty to 30 minutes a day from about 32 inches (80 cm) is generally sufficient.

4 A spotlight is used for diurnal turtles in the morning and afternoon, in all about six hours per day. It produces a temperature of about 104°F (40°C) on the bottom.

38°C ← → 23°C

The Right Accommodations

Aquatic turtles have different lifestyles. This has implications for their accommodations. There are three possibilities.

› **Aquaterrariums for land dwellers** with a small area of water and a larger land section.

› **Aquariums for aquatic turtles** that don't swim well, with a water depth equal to twice the breadth of the shell, plus a suspended land portion.

› **Aquariums for aquatic species** that swim well, with deep water (around 16 to 20 inches / 40–50 cm) and a suspended land portion.

An Aquaterrarium

This is appropriate for such turtles as the Yellow-margined Painted Turtle and the Chinese Three-keeled Turtle. As adult turtles they need a large land portion (see Profiles on pages 17 and 21). You can partition the tank into two halves using a plate of Plexiglas as wide as the tank and held in place with aquarium silicone. The water portion is on one side of the dividing wall, and the land portion is set up on the other side. You can find the appropriate water depth in the profiles. Set up the land portion

In this well-set-up aquaterrarium for land-dwelling aquatic turtles, a temperature gradient makes it possible for the turtle to select its preferred temperature.

in such a way that the top surface of the land is about an inch (2.5 cm) higher than the water portion. The dividing wall should be at least 2 inches (5 cm) above the water level. You can even let it project a good 2¾ inches (7 cm) above the land. The advantage is that the water is protected from getting dirty when the turtle is digging on the land. But the turtle always needs a comfortable access onto land from the water. You can provide this by cutting a passageway through the dividing wall wider than the turtle's shell. A ramp comes up out of the water and allows your turtle to climb onto the land portion.

(On page 36 you will see how to set up the land portion.)

Aquariums for Poor Swimmers

This involves an aquarium with shallow water. Your turtle runs under water rather than swimming. Thus, it must be able to reach the surface of the water at all times, without having to swim, in order to breathe. This is accomplished by putting in plenty of branches or a loop of sisal rope, where the turtle can easily get traction and climb. The climbing aids should have a diameter of at least 2 to 8 inches (5–20 cm).

With a little imagination you can make the access to the edge of the land portion both natural and comfortable for the turtle.

The water level is adjusted to the needs of the inhabitant, and it is indicated for each species in the profiles. The water in the setup must always be deeper than the turtle's breadth. That is the only way that it can turn back over if it ever rolls onto its back. If it can't do this, it will drown.

A flat shore area is ideal for baby Mud Turtles. You can create this by tipping the aquarium slightly and making the bottom slip-proof by putting in something like a sisal mat. Place the aquarium onto a board (with an underlay; see the tip on p. 30). Put one or two strips of wood under the side opposite the suction side for the filter. That way the water collects in the deepest area (see illustration,

p. 25); this should result in a water level of about 2 to 3 inches (5–7 cm).

Plants for the Water Portion: Pure carnivores don't bother robust aquarium plants such as egeria, Hornblatt, and thread algae, as long as they don't become bored. You can also put in plastic plants for cover and decoration. It's a good idea to consult with your pet shop owner to avoid poisonous plants.

Setting Up the Land Portion: The land portion consists of a standard plastic container, or you can glue together five sheets of eighth-inch (3 mm) Plexiglas. The size of the land portion is indicated in the profiles (see pp. 14–21). It is hung—much like a flower box on a balcony railing—with two U-shaped steel clamps (from a hardware store), separated from the front and back panes by a sixteenth or an eighth of an inch (2–3 mm). Put some foam under the clamps to protect the edge of the glass. Loose installation simplifies subsequent maintenance. The underside of the land portion can go into the water up to about 2 inches (5 cm), or be suspended over the surface of the water to take up as little swimming room as possible. The area under the land portion serves as a convenient hiding place.

An aquarium for poor swimmers has climbing aids under the water: The land portion is suspended loosely; cork bark tubes provide both access to land and hiding places.

Your turtle will climb onto the land portion for basking and for laying eggs. The side walls must be high enough so that your turtle can leave it only to go safely to the water. The ground consists of a mixture of half sand and half deciduous leaf litter, and is always kept "misty damp."

To serve as an exit from the water, put in a gradual ramp in the form of a thick branch. The ramp or the land portion is heated to 104°F (40°C) with a spotlight, unless something else is specified in the profiles on pages 14 through 21.

In the profiles I have recommended a cork tube as an aid for small "climbers"; it can be set up at an angle in front of the land portion. Glue the tube horizontally between the front and back panes of the tank. To keep it from slipping, attach it with wire to the metal clamps for the land portion. The tube sticks out about a third over the surface of the water to produce an air space inside. The tube is cut lengthwise under the water, and is open along the cut. This is a place where the turtle can withdraw to and still easily get air. Branches will make it easier for the turtle to climb up. Before putting in the cork tube, cut three air holes about ½ inch (1 cm) wide and 2 inches (5 cm) long into it so that plenty of fresh air can always get in.

Plants for the Land Portion: Good choices for greenery are space-saving hanging plants that hang from the edge of the tank and provide cover, such as Ficus pumila, philodendron, and ferns.

Aquariums for Good Swimmers

Fill the tank with water according to the specifications in the profiles (see pp. 14–21), and suspend the land portion inside as high as possible.

Setting Up the Water Space: Swimmers need

Decorative plants: Your turtle cannot reach them outside the tank, and yet lives in a natural environment.

lots of open room to swim. They like to use a piece of root projecting over the water for basking. It must always be possible to jump from the sunning place into deep water without danger of injury.

The current will bring together floating dried pieces of reeds, leaves from cattails, or pine bark in calm areas to produce floating islands that provide cover and give the aquarium a natural touch.

Important: The water must be kept at a level where the turtle cannot reach the rim of the aquarium and climb out.

Land Portion: This is suspended as described on page 36. This is where the turtles sun themselves and the females lay their eggs. Page 36 also tells you how to set up the land portion and create an access to it, so that your turtles have an appropriate environment.

A Sunny Paradise for Aquatic Turtles

There is nothing better for your turtle than a life in natural sunlight and in your pond, an environment full of living food animals and plants. But in many temperate zones keeping a turtle outdoors is possible only in the months of June through August. With a glass house you can extend that time by one to three months. Please pay attention to my recommendations in the profiles on keeping a turtle outdoors.

An Outdoor Enclosure in the Yard

The Ideal Shape and Location: The best option is a pond with a diameter of about 20 feet (6 m). If you don't have enough space, it could be smaller, since that is always better than no pond at all. It should always receive as much full sunlight as possible.

The backyard pond as an adventure space: Without a glass house your turtle can live here from June through August in most temperate zones.

I recommend a round pond lined with plastic sheeting with a flat shore area about 6 feet (2 m) wide. There should be an area in the middle of the pond about 3 feet (1 m) deep and 6 feet (2 m) across. The shore area should have an incline of about 7 degrees; toward the middle, the angle should be 45 to 50 degrees. This type of pond will hold a little more than 1,500 gallons (5,600 L) of water, including nearly 1,100 gallons (4,000 L) near the shore, where the water can warm up quickly in the sun.

Use black pond liner, which remains exposed at the edges. The black color encourages warming in the sun. In the center, plant cattails or reeds in a basin filled with sand; around this group, in an area of calm water, put in some old logs to serve as islands for basking. You can likewise decorate the shallow water area with this type of wood. In a short time your pond will become covered with algae, and even the sheeting will be covered with a thin coating of lime. With pure meat eaters you can still decorate the pond with plants placed in baskets. All other turtles eat the plants (except for reeds and cattails).

Technical Equipment: If you keep no more than three turtles in this pond, a filter generally is not necessary, for the compounds in the water can process the organic contaminants from the turtles.

If the contamination increases, you can remove the water from the middle—where most of the "trash" collects—for watering the garden, and put in fresh water (a partial water change). If you put in a pond filter, choose a pump that handles about 70

In this outdoor setup with a greenhouse and lowered water level, the glass house contains a hibernation basin and a tank for young turtles; the reed island provides cooling shade. The rest is set up for the best possible usage of solar energy and for warming the water.

to 140 gallons (250–500 L) per hour. Suck the water from the deepest point in the center and let it run back into the cluster of reeds.

Edging: The whole setup must be made secure by surrounding it with a palisade, fiber cement, or a rough timber fence at least 16 inches (40 cm) high. A building supplies store can give you advice about any necessary foundation if you want to put up a wall of concrete blocks. In order to keep the bound-

ary visually acceptable, you can lower the level of the pond or pile dirt up around the outside of the enclosure. If you have children, you should also put up a fence to keep the pond secure from anyone getting in and drowning.

Tip: If you use 75 or 100 feet (25–30 m) of black plastic hose as a return for the pump and lay it out in a spiral in a sunny spot, preferably on a sheet of black corrugated iron, you create a solar pond heater. The water flows through this setup and returns to the pond warm, even on overcast days.

A Glass House for Warming Up

The spring and fall in some temperate regions can temporarily be so cold that your turtle cannot reach its preferred body temperature inside the pond. The solution is a glass house in the form of a cold frame—or, even more conveniently for you, and roomier for the turtle—a small greenhouse. That way you can use a glass house to extend to May through September the outdoors time for all turtles that go on land, as long as the weather is good.

> **The Advantage of the Greenhouse Effect:** In the summer a closed glass house warms up even when the sky is overcast. Oftentimes the diffuse (scattered) radiation from the sun is all that it takes. The warming rays go through the glass panes, but cannot get out, so they raise the inside temperature. If the air temperature on the floor of the glass house doesn't get up to 86°F (30°C), help it with a spotlight that warms only the basking area up to 104°F (40°C). An adjustable, automatic ventilation flap in the roof protects against overheating, using standard thermal elements, in case you are caring for plants or young turtles in the glass house. In other words, the flap opens at a specific temperature.

> **The Advantage of the "Fun Bath" Principle:** This involves your turtle's being able to swim in and out the way it wants, making it easier for the turtle to regulate its body temperature. It can warm itself inside the glass house, and then go into the backyard pond to look for food. It will return to the warmth to digest its food.

Making a Glass House

With a little architectural imagination—and advice from an architect or a skilled mason—it is easy to construct this turtle's dream. You will need a standard cold frame or small greenhouse that you can place on a concrete foundation (using a pre-mix from a building supplies store).

The balcony setup is like an aquarium with a large land portion, and requires the same kind of care. In addition, it provides your turtle with all the advantages of being kept outdoors.

Important: You need to put the foundation into the pond before you put the sheeting into place, for the sheeting is placed over it; a pad between the sheeting and the concrete protects against damage.

The foundation has a 12 × 20 inch (30 × 50 cm) opening in the shallow water, about 2 inches (4–5 cm) below the surface, for the turtle to get through. (In the illustration on page 39 the water level is slightly lower for clarity.) Place the glass house onto the foundation. The lower edge is a little more than an inch (2.5 cm) under water. That prevents undesired heat loss. You can also leave out the foundation under the long side of the glass house in the water, and set up a variable opening for the turtle. Close up the opening under water with bricks set loosely into place up to the way through. If you let sand float into the joints between the bricks, the warm water that now gets heated inside also can't flow out.

Your turtle will quickly learn where the entryway is. At the beginning you can also show it how to find the entry with a "guide" in the form of an underwater row of stones or a branch to follow. Usually all it takes is spreading some food in the water inside the glass house to help your turtle sniff out the correct way.

A Mini Pond on a Terrace or a Balcony

Do you have no yard, but a sunny terrace or balcony? You can also set up an appropriate body of water for your turtle there (see the Expert Tips at right).

The setup contains the same elements as the indoor one, based on the turtle's biology, but there is no illumination. Here too you must use a fairly high border to keep the turtle from getting out.

An Outdoor Setup on the Balcony

TIPS FROM THE
TURTLE EXPERT
Dr. Hartmut Wilke

1. The setup is made from pressure-treated fence boards from a building supplies store. The rear is higher than the front, so the sides slope toward the front.

2. Line the setup with pond sheeting. Punch holes 4 inches (10 cm) apart in the sheeting so that any seepage can get out.

3. Put in a mortar tub for a pond, and in its bottom, the return for the filter, with a valve. Use the information in the profiles to adjust the water level and the decorations. Then fill the box from bottom to top as follows: 8 inches (20 cm) expanded clay (from a garden shop), a root barrier, and deciduous leaf litter just high enough to keep the turtle from reaching the edge.

4. Add plants and decorations to the water portion as described on pages 36 and 37.

5. Two Plexiglas sheets make a good cover. To keep the heat from building up you can raise one of the panes, or use a standard thermal element to raise and lower it. You can shade the other one with a piece of matting.

Fit and Healthy

In order to feel good in your care, your aquatic turtle has other needs in addition to the proper food. It also wants to satisfy its natural needs. So grant its wishes for a setup that is always clean, for undisturbed rest—and, if you have a female, for a place to lay eggs.

Healthy Nutrition for Aquatic Turtles

Most aquatic turtles give the impression that they are always hungry, and beg as soon as you come near them. The danger is that you will feel sorry for a turtle and overfeed it or give it an unbalanced diet. Young turtles react to this with poor, excessively fast growth and deformed shells. In addition, overweight is of course a threat.

The Right Diet

I chose the word *diet* intentionally, because that way you avoid overfeeding. The first step occurs inside your head. Simply ignore the begging behavior of your turtle. If the turtle swims over to you and wants food the moment you appear, this generally has nothing to do with its current need for protein; it does show, however, how quick to learn the turtle is.

By *diet* I mean that you provide all the necessary nutrients in appropriate amounts. In the wild, the great variety of food creatures in the water delivers the necessary nutrients. The menu includes crustaceans (water fleas), insects and their larvae (mosquito larvae, water bugs), mollusks (snails and mussels), carrion (fishes, mammals, birds), young fishes in general, amphibians, and tadpoles.

With age, many turtle species transition to a mixed diet in varying degrees (see profiles, pp. 14–21); in other words, they take in an equal amount of plant-based nutrients.

As much variety as there is on the menu in the wild, aquatic turtles can hardly overeat on water fleas and mosquito larvae, and a fat, dead pike-perch doesn't come in front of their noses every day.

If you are now thinking that a healthy feeding plan for an aquatic turtle is very demanding, I can put your fears to rest. It involves only minor effort and a clearly defined program.

The Basic Food

The basic food comes from the pet food industry.

Young Turtles: For them it consists exclusively of a meat diet in the form of freeze-dried crustaceans (*Gammarus pules*, water fleas), insects, and insect larvae (in a "mix"). If your baby turtle doesn't accept this, feed it live food, for example, red Chironomidae larvae, young crickets, and water fleas. Tubifex, red sludge worms, are generally seriously contaminated with heavy metals (from the bottom of the body of water) because of their lifestyle; as a result, before using them for feed you should soak them for three days. There are such things as *Enchitraeus*, small relatives of earthworms, which are available in pet shops year-round.

Growing Turtles at Least Two to Three Months Old: These turtles get the same food as young turtles, but only about 60 percent of their daily ration. The remaining 40 percent consists of whole (dead) fishes, such as guppies and bait fishes used by anglers, which are given as a supplement to satisfy hunger. If your turtle has difficulty with whole fishes, it's best to cut them up into bite-sized pieces.

Adult Turtles that Eat Only Meat: Thirty percent of their food consists of whole fishes, 10 percent of whole, frozen newborn mice that you warm to water temperature after thawing, 30 percent of pure beef heart with a pinch of calcium—if the turtle has no cuttlefish shell—or freshwater fish such as pike-perch, both cut into thin strips, and 30 percent from freeze-dried small crustaceans and

The River Cooter prefers to eat plants. Your backyard pond won't satisfy its appetite; you will have to provide supplemental feedings.

A Food Source in the Outdoor Setup

In order to provide live food at all times, you can make a small compost pile inside the outdoor setup, preferably in a partially shaded area. Surround it with rotten, untreated wood by placing a couple of boards or strips at the bottom of the mound. Small creatures of all kinds such as isopods, earthworms, grubs, bugs, and millipedes will take up residence in it.

LAND SPECIES: Land-dwelling turtles, such as the Yellow-margined Painted Turtle, will soon go there to hunt.

AQUATIC SPECIES: Throw the collected animal life into the water for species that rarely go onto land.

insects. Don't give all components every day, but alternate on a daily basis and offer fish, then mice, and then small crustaceans.

Adult Omnivores to Near Vegetarians: They generally get a half portion or more of the mixture for adult meat eaters, depending on the specifications in the profiles (see pp. 14–21). The remaining portion consists of water plants from the backyard pond and/or soft weeds, such as chickweed, clover, dandelion leaves (from the yard), and arugula (from a store).

Added Value Through Natural Foods

I recommend this practice. Replace part or all of the preserved food portion with live and fresh food.
❯ In the backyard pond you can raise egeria, hornwort, and water snails.
❯ It is easy to breed guppies in an aquarium. This applies also to crickets and young walking sticks (from a pet shop), as long as they can't get out of the aquarium.
❯ Black mosquito larvae will automatically appear in a pan containing rainwater.
❯ In other bodies of water you can catch live food in the traditional manner using a net. But before you do, check to be sure there are no restrictions (such as private property, fishing prohibitions, and so on).
❯ Your yard is a productive source of slugs and snails of all types, earthworms, millipedes, and isopods (see the tip at left).

Live Food from a Pet Shop: If you don't have a yard, you can buy live food in a pet shop. There you will find such things as a breeding kit for Japanese water fleas and information about how to proceed. In addition you can get larvae of mealworms and darkling beetles. They contain lots of fat but not many vitamins. Use them only occasionally to give your turtle something to do, and in no case as the foundation for a diet.

Always lying in wait: Your turtle quickly learns to keep an eye on the random food dispenser, which "rains" treats. This is a good way for the turtle to keep busy.

Commercially Manufactured Foods for Aquatic Turtles

If you don't want to prepare the food yourself, you can also use commercially manufactured food from a pet shop. Since the food is intended to suit a large number of species, it is formulated "comprehensively" and may not always meet the dietary specifications in this handbook. Usually the food is made up of *Gammarus pulex*, mollusks, insects, and "animal by-products" with a protein content of around 40 to 50 percent and a fat content of 4 to 5 percent.

In addition, the food should contain calcium and phosphorus, ideally more calcium. If you don't see

1 Crickets are a valuable component in the broad food spectrum of an aquatic turtle. They are easy to breed at home.

2 Chickweed (photo) and egeria are easy to grow. They provide welcome variety in your turtle's menu.

any information about the calcium and phosphorus content, I recommend using this food only for "amusement" purposes on the fasting days, and in no case for raising young turtles or as a sole food source for adult turtles.

Making Prepared Foods Yourself

I first encountered the idea of producing turtle food with all the required ingredients into an "aspic" in the early 1970s at a zoo. This type of food also crops up in many variations in the literature. The mixture I recommend carefully follows the scientifically calculated "original recipe" and contains everything required for healthy nutrition. You can alter the taste by changing the portion of squid, mussels, and fresh shrimp. Your turtle will like that.

In a single work session you can produce enough turtle food for three to six months, and it can easily be divided into portions and fed to the turtle by a replacement caregiver. For food conservation reasons the mixture should be used up after six months.

Basic Recipe

> 14 ounces (400 g) freshwater fish, whole
> 7 ounces (200 g) beef heart
> 7 ounces (200 g) squid, in natural state
> 10 ounces (300 g) shrimp or krill meal with 50 percent protein content (from feed store)
> two eggs with shells (raw)
> shells from two raw or boiled eggs, or half a cuttlefish shell
> up to 7 ounces (200 g) of "greens"—depending on your turtle's requirements—such as stinging nettle leaves, arugula, clover, chickweed, or carrots, unpeeled apples, cooked rice, or cornmeal.

Preparation: Wash all ingredients in running water, and then puree everything with a little water, the meat separately from the rest of the ingredients, in a high-speed mixer (blender), into a honey-like liquid broth. Mix everything together and heat it to 176°F (80°C) (use a thermometer!). Keep stirring the broth and let it cool down to 122 to 140°F (50–60°C), and add high-quality food gelatin (from a grocery store) and a vitamin and mineral preparation such as Corvimin or Davinova in accordance with your veterinarian's instructions.

Good-quality gelatin is important, for otherwise the food will not be solid enough and will subsequently deteriorate in the water. Pour the preparation into a baking pan to solidify. Then cut it into daily rations keyed to the size and the appetite of your turtle; freeze these in plastic bags and thaw them as needed. The aspic is used only as a supplemental food source for omnivores and turtles that are primarily vegetarians, and the plant material is fed to them fresh.

Nutritional Supplements

Calcium: You should always have this available in the form of cuttlefish shell, ground mussel shells (from a pet shop), or ground shells from boiled eggs. Your turtle can eat it as desired. The need for calcium is particularly high in young turtles and in females during the egg-formation phase.

Vitamins and Trace Elements: These probably are not necessary if your turtle gets live food and UV light, and lives outdoors during the summer. Give it vitamins only after consultation with your veterinarian.

Proper **Feeding**

TIPS FROM THE
TURTLE EXPERT
Dr. Hartmut Wilke

HOW OFTEN SHOULD I FEED MY TURTLE?
Young turtles get their food spread over the whole day. As they grow older, feed the turtles just once or twice a day. Every other day observe a day of "fasting" in which it gets only a small hunk of commercial food or a few water fleas. Sexually mature females are fed daily when they are producing eggs, and up to a month after laying their last batch of eggs for the season.

WHEN SHOULD I FEED IT? Feed your turtle during its active times. In other words,
> turtles that are active during the day should be fed after their sunbath in the morning, and in the late afternoon.
> turtles that are active at twilight should be fed in the half light of morning and evening.

HOW MUCH SHOULD I FEED? Let the turtle fast for one day. Then weigh or measure the amount of food you intend to give. As soon as your turtle slows down or becomes more selective in its eating, weigh the remainder and subtract the result from the original weight. From then on, feed only half the amount consumed in the experiment.

Care Basics

Your turtle will get the best care if you comply with all the advice in this handbook. Careful selection of food and appropriate feeding times, combined with the right space, temperature, and lighting, plus the opportunity to experience the rhythm of individual days and years, are the essential features of care. Your turtle will remain vital and grow up healthy. Under improper conditions it can become sick. A regular, yearly preventive health check (see p. 57) is still a good idea.

Taking Care of the Setup

Keep the land portion of the turtle setup in hygienically perfect condition by removing food remains and droppings every day.

Partial Water Change: You will rarely find the droppings in solid form in the water, but the crushed, solid components still collect either in the filter or as "rot" on the floor of the tank, commonly in the same places. You can suck up the decayed material with a hose by siphoning it into a bucket. For hygienic reasons, don't suck on the hose with your mouth, but rather fill up the hose by dipping it into the tank with aquarium water. Then close off the end of the hose with your thumb and open it in the bucket, which is placed lower than the water level in the tank. The water will flow into the bucket. This way you can change 30 to 50 percent of the aquarium water and replace it with tap water at the same temperature.

Complete Water Change and Filter Care: The water also contains waste materials from urine, droppings, and dissolving leftover food. If these wastes get out of control, the bacteria that break them down can become so numerous that you can see them as a milky haze in the water. Then it's time to change the entire water and rinse the filter. Remove the water as described above and suck the decayed material out of the corners and off the

Regular cleaning of your setup is important for general hygiene, the turtle's health, and taking the strain off the filter.

bottom. Clean the roots and glass panes with a sponge. The contamination will flow out with the water. Always rinse the filter with clear water to avoid harming the useful microbes that live in it and recondition the water. Then bring the new water up to the temperature previously measured in the old water and fill the tank. Finally you can put the turtle back in.

Water Change Frequency: How often you change the water depends on the stress from urine, droppings, and leftover food. In my experience, a single turtle calls for a rhythm in which a partial water change is done every week, and a complete water change every two to three months. While you are cleaning, place the turtle onto the land portion or into the quarantine aquarium.

Notice: Light discoloration from bogwood and peat extracts is quite harmless, and even advantageous for many turtles that like low light. Leaf litter that ends up in the water when a turtle digs around is also harmless, even if it clouds the water.

Cleaning the Outdoor Setup

Empty the backyard pond once a year in November, using a pump for dirty water and simultaneously stirring up the decayed material. Then fill up the pond again. Drifting leaves commonly collect at the edge of the shore, where they can be removed. You don't need to be concerned about small life forms, for your turtle has already taken care of them during the summer.

Advice on the **Internet**

TIPS FROM THE
TURTLE EXPERT
Dr. Hartmut Wilke

GOOD INFORMATION: You can find informative and factual web sites with the most recent scientific information from the recognized national turtle organizations (see Addresses, p. 62). There you will also find many exciting links to museums, university departments, and research stations. Private English-language home pages also contain neat summaries of scientific knowledge about specific species.

SUSPECT INFORMATION: Because anyone can write practically anything on the Internet in any way they want, you may also come across some "crusaders." If you have any doubts about the statements, you should get confirmation from the recommended web pages or draw comparisons to the specialized literature.

CHECKING INFORMATION: I also recommend checking statements against scientific standards; if a statement is supported and verified by a series of experiments, then you can believe it. If it is not, it is best considered a working hypothesis.

Crucial Hibernation

Species that live in areas where the winter is cold take a rest in the winter. In this time the creatures rest with lowered body temperatures and in special hiding places. Whether or not your turtle rests in the winter is specified in the profiles (see pp. 14–21). If your turtle needs a winter rest, you will be able to tell by its behavior when the days grow shorter in September and October. The turtle will eat significantly less or not at all, empty its intestine to a major extent, and stop moving.

Introduction to Hibernation

Before your turtle goes into hibernation, it is important that you

❯ have the creature checked by the veterinarian in August, or at least have a stool sample checked for worms. All treatments should be successfully completed by the end of September;

❯ continually adjust the duration of the lighting to the length of the day outdoors;

❯ lower the temperature of the water and air in three or four stages, each of which lasts a week, by a good two to three degrees Centigrade, at the first signs of a need to take a winter rest, such as reduced food intake. Altogether that amounts to 10 to 12 degrees Centigrade. You thus create a water temperature of 57 to 61°F (14–16°C) and an air temperature of 64°F (18°C).

Hibernation in Water

In the profiles (see pp. 14–21) you can find out whether your turtle spends the winter on the bottom of a body of water. If so, it will need a resting place under water in the aquarium.

You need special winter quarters for this. This can be either a concrete basin that you put into the cellar, or a plastic container with a lid in the refrig-

The European Swamp Turtle likes to spend the winter in the wild buried under roots in the mud. Often several turtles collect in the same spot.

erator. The plastic container should be at least 50 percent wider and longer than the turtle's shell is long. The turtle must be able to turn around easily in the container. When the turtle stands up straight, it must not be able to reach the lid. The turtle needs this space for stored breathing air; with containers that close tightly, five to ten holes a half-inch (1 cm) in diameter in the lid will let the air flow in.

Fill the concrete tray or container with water to the point where your turtle can easily get air when it is resting on the bottom. Replace the mulch that occurs in natural waters with foam peanuts about an inch (2.5 cm) long. The turtle will feel secure among them. Cover 95 percent of the concrete tray with a board to keep the light out. The containers spend the winter in the temperature range recommended for your turtle.

Hibernation on Land

Many species hibernate on land. They climb up onto the land portion and look for a place to spend the winter. Put these turtles into a hibernation tank that you fill three-quarters full—not with water, but with a moist mixture of deciduous leaf litter and bark mulch in even proportions. *Moist* means 90 percent relative humidity, not wet. The tank has a cover of 2-inch-square (5 × 5 cm) mesh. In this type of hibernation tank there is a very great danger that the turtle will become dehydrated. The Common Musk Turtle is particularly sensitive to this. The best way to avoid dehydration is to add water to the edge of the tank. Never pour it onto the turtle itself. A hygrometer should be next to the turtle in a plastic container with holes in it, and it must always show 90 percent relative humidity (calibrate it every year).

Provide security for hibernation by replacing the natural mud bed with foam packing pellets and by darkening the tank.

Careful: **Spending the Winter in the Pond**

You may encounter recommendations that give the impression that aquatic turtles can spend the winter in the backyard pond without adverse consequences. This is not true.

EUROPEAN POND TURTLE: Even though this species should be appropriate for this in certain regions where it occurs naturally, I would leave this experiment to experts with lots of experience.

ALL OTHER SPECIES: In many temperate regions the spring and fall are too changeable and cold for too long, and global climate change is another factor. Unfortunately, in practice too many deaths continually verify this.

You can let your turtle spend the winter in a box rather than the tank, as it would be used for a land turtle. The hibernation box has an advantage in the form of a more consistent climate.

Things to Do During the Winter Rest

Checks and Water Care: Examine your turtle every three to five days. If it is healthy, the sudden light will not disturb it. If the water is clear and free of bubbles, it does not need to be changed. If necessary (milky cloudiness), cool the clean replacement water to the appropriate temperature before a change. Turtles that spend the winter on land

need to be checked only once a week because of the stable microclimate.

Illness During Hibernation: It can happen that during the winter rest your turtle will become active sooner than anticipated, and without obvious reason. One evident reason would be a significant, early warming-up of the winter quarters. If you have doubts, interrupt the winter rest as described below and take your turtle to a veterinarian. Thereafter the turtle must be cared for until healthy according to the veterinarian's recommendations and under normal living conditions in its setup, or preferably in the quarantine aquarium.

Ending the Winter Rest

After the hibernation time indicated in the profiles has gone by, bring the container with the turtle back into a bright room at 65 to 68°F (18–20°C) and let the light back in. As the temperature increases, your turtle will become increasingly active. Then put the turtle into its setup at the same temperature. Now raise the temperature of the air and water every two days by about two degrees Centigrade until you get them up to the normal temperatures specified in the profiles. After about a week the turtle will begin eating.

Because of their wide north-south distribution, among Yellow-margined Painted Turtles there are individuals that hibernate at 39 to 45°F (4–7°C) or at around 59°F (15°C). Test your turtle with the help of the temperature gradient.

The Proper Living Conditions

If you observe a few rules right from the beginning, it won't take your turtle long to feel that it's in good hands. That way you also provide your pet with its best chances for good health and vitality.

Good Idea

(+) Always keep the water for your turtle up to the best standards for aquarium water—as if you were taking care of fishes.

(+) Feed as great a variety of foods as possible, using predominantly fresh food.

(+) Have the yearly routine health check done in August. That way any necessary treatment can generally be concluded before the winter rest.

(+) Observe the specifications for winter rest also for baby turtles.

Bad Idea

(−) Do not substitute the addition of chemical substances such as a water improver for responsible care for water quality, and filter and water changes.

(−) In a temperate climate, do not keep aquatic turtles in a backyard pond year-round, and don't let them spend the winter there without carefully checking on them.

(−) Do not give your turtle only commercially manufactured food.

(−) Do not substitute vitamins for time spent on land and UV lighting.

(−) Do not give your turtle vitamins at your discretion without consulting a veterinarian, especially vitamins A and D.

Breeding Aquatic Turtles

Around fifty years ago the decline of many turtle species into the status of "threatened with extinction" began. Habitat destruction by humans and removal from the wild for food and as pets are still a threat today. Uncontrolled abandonment by anxious enthusiasts of animals that have grown too large is a threat to the ecosystem. Even though protecting the biotope is still the first-choice remedy, breeding aquatic turtles in captivity is a good contribution to species protection, for it may spell the end of removal from the wild.

For this reason, in this handbook I recommend only species that can reproduce in our latitudes. If possible you should also choose your turtle from these species. This increases the chance of locating healthy animals. If you want to breed your own turtles, there are advantages to putting a mating pair together. Because you know the parents, you can choose offspring from different breeding lines that are not related to one another. That way you prevent inbreeding and help to continue genetically intact breeding lines.

Notice: There are babies and crosses of Painted Turtles and Sliders available on the market. There is nothing wrong with keeping this type of turtle by itself for a long time, and perhaps freeing it from the pound at an animal shelter. However, I implore you not to use such mongrels for breeding.

National herpetological (reptile) organizations in many countries (see Addresses, p. 62) work to keep breeding lines pure and maintain breeding registries. You can locate them through your regional terrarium association. Until you can hold your first baby turtles in your hands, the following basics of courtship, mating, and egg laying should be observed.

This Yellow-margined Painted Turtle is a cute baby. In a couple of years, though, it will turn into an 8–11-inch (20–28 cm) turtle.

Prerequisites for Mating: In order to produce young, you need a mating pair. Keep the partners separated throughout the year by giving each one its own enclosure. If you don't have that much space, you can join a breeding cooperative, lend the turtle partner for the short breeding time, and share the offspring.

Courtship and Mating

In the mating season, which generally begins after the winter rest, or in the spring, put the turtles together under your constant supervision. Two sexually mature, healthy turtles—preferably hormonally well disposed toward each other through hibernation—will generally mate within an hour. Sometimes you may have to be patient for a couple of days. If the partners get along, all you have to do is check in from time to time to see if everything is in order. Courtship and mating of aquatic turtles, with few exceptions, such as the Yellow-margined Box Turtle, takes place in the water.

Interesting Courtship Rituals: This will be the reward for your patience. The male Painted Turtles, Sliders, and Red-bellied Short-necked Turtles are real artists in "worshipping" their loved one. Painted Turtles tremble with both front legs; Red-bellied Short-necked Turtles (see p. 15) fan with just one front leg—a display that you will enjoy as a spectator. In addition, the males exhibit a ritualized nodding of the head before they swim up behind the female to mate. With Mud Turtles the rituals are not so stylized. Very frequently they reach their goal spontaneously.

After mating—with compatible turtles, after two to four days—separate the male from the female for the rest of the year. If the partners don't get along, separate them immediately.

Mating Snake-necked Turtles put on an impressive show. With this species mating usually goes smoothly.

Egg Laying and Maturation

After successful mating in the spring, the female lays her eggs within a few weeks. By then she needs somewhere to lay her eggs, that is, a place on land that you create with a mixture of deciduous leaf litter and sand in even proportions. Now warm this place all day long with the spotlight to a ground temperature of 93 to 97°F (34–36°C). There, or a little to one side, the turtle will bury her eggs.

In addition you now need a simple, standard incubator, which you use according to the instructions. Dig up the eggs and bed them as directed in vermiculite (from a pet shop) and water in equal proportions by weight. That way you create a relative humidity of 90 to 95 percent inside the incubator. In the wild, the embryos have to survive the fluctuations in temperature and moisture. The incubation temperature generally is around 82°F (28°C), but it may fluctuate for a few days between 77 and 86°F (25–30°C). With many turtle species, sex is determined by the brood temperature. (For more information on this, check any number of sites online.)

Embryo Development and Hatching

A fertilized egg gains weight with time; in addition, you can use a desk lamp to shine through the inside of the egg to see blood vessels, and later on the embryo as a dark spot. Take the egg between your thumb and index finger and blot out excess light with your hand. With soft-shelled eggs, at the beginning of development you will also see a growing, lighter "belly band" around the middle of the shell. Colors on the eggshell (often reddish or brownish) are of no consequence. Healthy embryos subjected to temporary fluctuations in temperature and humidity can get by all right, but weakened ones can die even under the best of brooding conditions.

After the species-specific incubation, which also depends on the brood temperature, the young turtle hatches with the help of its "egg tooth." It can take up to three days for it to leave the shell entirely. Any leftover egg yolk about the size of a pea will degenerate (be used up) in about a week. After hatching, place both good and poor swimmers separately into shallow, very clean water until the process is complete.

Raising Young Turtles

Young aquatic turtles prefer to live in the water and are raised separated from their parents. Poor swimmers are put into very shallow water. In the first four to eight weeks it's best to feed the babies live water fleas, mosquito larvae, and young earthworms, which will satisfy the turtles' desire to hunt. Later you can slowly transition to the prescribed diet (see p. 44) in the form of frozen food and small, freshly killed fishes.

If the Striped Mud Turtle lays viable eggs for you, you have graduated from the ranks of beginners!

Health Precautions and Treating Diseases

Perfect hygiene (see p. 48) and observing the technical instructions on organizing the individual terrarium and the climate as provided in this handbook are the best preconditions for keeping your turtle healthy for life—provided that you also take seriously the instructions for proper nutrition (see p. 43). Still, it may happen that your turtle falls ill. In the following paragraphs I describe a few symptoms of illnesses (according to Renate Keil, DVM) that warrant your immediately taking the turtle to a veterinarian. Treatments should be done only in accordance with the veterinarian's advice, especially with respect to using antibiotics and vitamins.

Difficulty Breathing

Symptoms: The turtle spends most of its time on land, stretches its neck far forward, opens its mouth, and makes peeping, moaning, or snoring noises. It also keeps lowering its head in fatigue.
Possible Causes: Lung infection; constipation; egg binding; gas in stomach or intestines; bladder stone or clumps of uric acid that prevent emptying the bladder; edema from kidney or heart disease.
Treatment: At all costs avoid forcibly warming up the turtle; stimulating its metabolism could prove life threatening. Get the turtle to a veterinarian immediately.

Lung Infection

Symptoms: Difficulty breathing (see above), swimming off kilter, uncommonly frequent sessions under the spotlight. Don't confuse this with pregnant females, which also sun themselves a lot, but behave differently from a sick turtle.

Possible Causes: Draft, an air temperature cooler than the water temperature, keeping the turtle on the floor.
Treatment: By a veterinarian, only after taking X-rays to confirm the diagnosis.

Herpes

Symptoms: Coatings in the mouth that interfere with breathing, which, however, may also occur with fungal or bacterial infections.
Possible Causes: The herpes virus, which remains in the body for life, can lead to illness, usually in stressful situations, and can be unambiguously detected only through examinations in special laboratories.
Treatment: By a veterinarian. Only the accompanying infections can be treated. Herpes is usually fatal in turtles. Only immediate quarantine, hygiene, and disinfection measures can save the remaining stock.

Health Check

ONCE A WEEK: Look over your turtle carefully, including the underside, in accordance with the chart on page 58.

DAILY: Check the turtle's overall condition. That way you detect illnesses early and improve the chances of recovery. Eventually you will be able to get an idea of your turtle's condition with a brief glance.

Detecting **Diseases**

	SYMPTOMS
SHELL / YOUNG TURTLE	Healthy: firm and elastic like a thumbnail. Sick: soft and deformable, like a dinner roll.
SHELL / OLD TURTLE	Healthy: hard and firm, all horn plates free from damage. Sick: firm, but deformed; bumpy plates; holes, especially in the bottom shell; pink spots.
SKIN	Healthy: soft and leathery, smooth and elastic. Sick: bark-like; infected injuries; painful swellings; peeling at throat and cloaca area.
ANAL REGION	Healthy: clean, free of injury. Sick: injuries, bleeding wounds.
EYES	Healthy: clear, wide open. Sick: cornea cloudy; swollen, closed eyelids.
BREATHING PASSAGES	Healthy: silent breathing. Sick: raspy breathing, breathing with open mouth, swims off kilter.
MOVEMENT ON LAND	Healthy: uses all legs equally for movement. Sick: Back legs don't move much, or drag; the turtle "hangs" lower in the rear.
BEHAVIOR	Healthy: when the turtle is picked up, it resists forcefully. Sick: appears tired, apathetic.

Swollen Eyes

Symptoms: The eyelids are swollen, and the turtles cannot open their eyes.

Possible Causes: Draft, bacterially contaminated aquarium water, foreign object in eye, injuries, vitamin A deficiency.

Treatment: Only by veterinarian.

Note: All vitamin preparations that contain vitamins A and D must be administered in proportion to the turtle's body weight. In the wrong doses, they can cause extremely serious poisoning, which can lead to the dissolution of the epidermis.

Swollen Eardrum

Symptoms: The eardrum, between the mandibular joint and the eye, bulges outward (in a pea shape) quite prominently.

Possible Causes: Inner ear infection, inner pus accumulation.

Treatment: Only surgically by a veterinarian; a vitamin A deficiency may also play a role in this case.

Soft Shell

Symptoms: The shell becomes soft; bleeding occurs in the seams.

Possible Causes: Vitamin D_3 poisoning or vitamin D_3/calcium deficiency.

Treatment: Only by veterinarian; UV illumination and doses of lime; don't keep on sand or gravel, for the turtle will ingest too much of these when ill and suffer constipation or death.

Injuries to Shell

Symptoms: Superficial abrasions that may extend deeper into the bones.

Possible Causes: Usually mechanical injuries connected to being kept cool and continually damp, lack of a sunning place at 104°F (40°C), secondary infection.

Treatment: Surface shell abrasions are harmless. But go to the veterinarian if the wound goes down to the bone.

Shell Deformities

Symptoms: Caving in of the top shell or pyramid-shaped swelling of individual horn plates, especially in the growth phase of young turtles.

Possible Causes: Improper nutrition, especially with young turtles; vitamin D3 / calcium deficiency.

Treatment: By veterinarian. Also put in a UV lamp and provide calcium.

Heightened restlessness in females, especially on land (egg binding)

Symptoms: A sexually mature female may run around restlessly all day and dig holes. Frequently the soles of the feet get worn right through! See also "Difficulty Breathing."

Possible Causes: Physiological or anatomical reasons.

Treatment: By veterinarian, after taking an X-ray.

The Snake-necked Turtles belong to the genus of Side-necked Turtles because they tuck their head to the side in their shell. Clean water is also vitally important to them.

INDEX

Page numbers in **bold print** refer to illustrations.

Addresses

There are many organizations for turtle enthusiasts. The easiest way to locate them is to search online; a number of Internet sites are mentioned below.

The organizations named below can provide information about clubs for enthusiasts of different species of turtles. If you opt for collaboration, it may simplify things for you to join a breeding association. Such an association will also help you find the nearest terrarium club.

Important Notice

> **Electrical devices:** The electrical devices for terrarium care described in this book must be properly grounded. Be aware of the dangers in dealing with electrical devices and cords, especially in conjunction with water.

> **Hygiene:** Pay strict attention to your personal hygiene and wash your hands after coming into contact with these creatures.

Turtles on the Internet

www.reptilechannel.com/turtles-and-tortoises/default.aspx

www.nytts.org. The New York Turtle and Tortoise Society

www.sdturtle.org. The San Diego Turtle and Tortoise Society

www.matts-turtles.org. The Mid-Atlantic Turtle & Tortoise Society

www.turtleforum.com

www.boxturtlesite.info The place to learn about box turtles.

www.tortoise.org. The California Turtle & Tortoise Club

www.geocities.com/heartland/village/7666/. The Chicago Turtle Club—for help in maintaining the well-being, safety, and environment of turtles and tortoises

Questions about Terrariums

You can get answers to your questions from your veterinarian and any of the turtle or herpetological associations mentioned in this book.

Books

Bartlett, R. D. and Patricia. *Aquatic Turtles: Sliders, Cooters, Painted, and Map Turtles.* Hauppauge, NY: Barron's Educational Series, 2003.

———. *Box Turtles: Facts and Advice on Care and Breeding.* Hauppauge, NY: Barron's Educational Series, 2001.

———. *Turtles and Tortoises—Complete Pet Owner's Manual.* Hauppauge, NY: Barron's Educational Series, 2006.

Cook, Tess. *Box Turtles—Complete Herp Care.* Neptune City, NJ: TFH Publications, 2004.

Cursen, Sarah. *Those Terrific Turtles.* Sarasota, FL: Pineapple Press, 2006.

Kirkpatrick, David. *Aquatic Turtles—Complete Herp Care.* Neptune City, NJ: TFH Publications, 2006.

Patterson, Jordan. *The Guide to Owning a Box Turtle.* Neptune City, NJ: TFH Publications, 2004.

Wilke, Hartmut. *Turtles—a Complete Pet Owner's Manual.* Hauppauge, NY: Barron's Educational Series, 2006.

Magazines

HerpDigest (free Internet magazine): www.herpdigest.org

About the Author

Dr. Hartmut Wilke is a biologist, and as director of the Exotarium of the Frankfurt Zoo (Germany) and of the Darmstadt Zoo (Germany), he has accumulated practical experience with turtles throughout his career. He regularly provides advice to turtle enthusiasts.

About the Photographer

Christine Steimer works as a freelance photographer and specializes in pet photography. She works for international book publishers, scientific periodicals, and advertising agencies.

Acknowledgment

The publisher and author are deeply grateful to Renate Keil, DVM, for the descriptions of diseases on pp. 57–59.

First edition translated from the German by Eric A. Bye.

English translation © Copyright 2009 by Barron's Educational Series, Inc.

Original title of the book in German is *Wasserschildkröten*.

© Copyright 2007 by Gräfe and Unzer Verlag, GmbH, Munich.

All inquiries should be addressed to:
Barron's Educational Series, Inc.
250 Wireless Boulevard
Hauppauge, New York 11788
www.barronseduc.com

Library of Congress Catalog Card No.
2008049694

ISBN-13: 978-0-7641-4191-1
ISBN-10: 0-7641-4191-0

Library of Congress Cataloging-in-Publication Data

Wilke, Hartmut, 1943-
　　[Wasserschildkröten. English]
　　Aquatic turtles / Hartmut Wilke ; photographs, Christine Steimer.
　　　　p. cm.
　　Includes bibliographical references and index.
　　ISBN-13: 978-0-7641-4191-1
　　ISBN-10: 0-7641-4191-0
　1. Turtles as pets.　　I. Title.

　SF459.T8W5613 2009
　639.3'92—dc22
　　　　　　　　　　2008049694

Printed in China
9 8 7 6 5 4 3 2 1

Photo Credits

Christine Steimer, except for Uwe Anders (pp. 38, 55), Ken Griffiths/NHPA (p. 18), and Chris Mattison/NHPA (p. 59).

Cover Photos

Christine Steimer.

Important Notice

If you are scratched or bitten by your turtle, you should consult a physician immediately.

The electrical equipment described in this book for use with terrariums must be of UL-listed design and construction. Keep in mind the hazards associated with the use of such electrical appliances and wiring, especially near water. The use of an electronic circuit breaker that will interrupt the flow of electricity if damage occurs to appliances or wiring is strongly recommended. A protective switch, which must be installed by a licensed electrician, serves the same purpose.

SOS–What to Do?

Eating Plants

PROBLEM: Now that my Painted Turtle is no longer a baby, it eats all the aquarium plants. **SUGGESTION**: Put in plastic plants, or do without plants altogether. But make sure that there are plenty of hiding places and opportunities for climbing.

Shell Damage?

PROBLEM: My Snake-necked Turtle suddenly loses large pieces of the horn plates from its top and bottom shells. **SUGGESTION:** Relax! If the turtle is not bleeding, there is no problem, for many aquatic turtles renew the outer layer of horn on their shells in this way. Even large pieces of skin can come off in the process without harm.

Weight Problems

PROBLEM: When the turtle pulls in its legs, the folds of skin bulge out of the shell like bubbles. **SUGGESTION:**Your turtle is too fat. Cut back on the food ration by 30 to 40 percent until the stored fat gets burned up. Have the turtle fast every other day.

The Turtle Is Too Big

PROBLEM: My Red-cheeked Painted Turtle is 10 inches (25 cm) long and too big. My setup is too small, and I don't have enough room to expand it. **SUGGESTION:** Look for someone in a national organization (see the addresses on p. 62) who will adopt the turtle. You can establish contact with members who might be able to take the turtle off your hands. Never simply let the turtle go! That would be cruel.

Vanished

PROBLEM: The turtle is nowhere to be seen in the backyard pond. **SUGGESTION**: If your turtle has vanished in the fall, it may have gone down for hibernation. Empty the pond at the end of November and let the turtle spend the winter in the cellar or the hothouse. Young turtles with shell lengths of around 3 inches (8 cm) or less are also in danger of being eaten by a cat, a crow, or a heron. To protect against birds, cover the pond with a bird net. For protection against land predators, the turtle needs a secure island in the middle of the pond for resting at night.